Also by Donna Goddard

Fiction

Waldmeer (Book 1 of Waldmeer)

Together (Book 2 of Waldmeer)

Circles of Separation (Book 3 of Waldmeer)

Faith (Book 4 of Waldmeer)

Pittown (Book 5 of Waldmeer)

Prana (Book 6 of Waldmeer)

Purnima (Book 7 of Waldmeer)

Nonfiction

The Love of Being Loving (Book 1 of Love and Devotion)

The Love of Devotion (Book 2 of Love and Devotion)

Love's Longing (Book 3 of Love and Devotion)

Touched by Love (Book 4 of Love and Devotion)

Dance: A Spiritual Affair (Book 1 of The Creative Spirit Series)

Writing: A Spiritual Voice (Book 2 of The Creative Spirit Series)

Strange Words: Poems and Prayers (Book 3 of The Creative Spirit Series)

Writing:

A Spiritual Voice

The Creative Spirit Series

Book 2

Donna Goddard

Contents

Part 2: Fiction – Friends with Different Names

East-West Lead 75

About the Author

Introduction

Writing: A Spiritual Voice is not a technical book. Of those, there are many wonderful ones. It is about tuning into the writer's spiritual voice. It is also about the personal and unique ways that my writing has developed due to the foremost goal of listening and responding to the Divine. In a sense, all good writers are spiritual because, if they are good, they are inspired. We are trying to make that link to individual inspiration more direct. If you are a spiritual student, as well as a writer, you will want to use your writing for spiritual purposes in the same way that we use everything to align and expand our spiritual being.

Writing is a long-term career. It takes a lot of time, money, perseverance, learning, and soul. Making a mark as a writer and having an influence in the world is a process which generally accelerates slowly.

1. Keep going.
2. Keep giving.
3. Remain true.
4. Trust your instincts.
5. Go with the flow.
6. Do your best.
7. Enjoy it.

If you know that the spiritual voice is in you, and you would like greater access to it as a writer, then *Writing: A Spiritual Voice* can help you to develop your capacity to hear and heed that voice.

The Creative Spirit Series

The Creative Spirit Series is a 3-book nonfiction series. The books are more meditations and personal thoughts on the creative process than how-to-do books. We don't have desires by accident. Good desires are planted in us because we are meant to follow them, explore them, wrestle with them, and have them form us. If we do this, and do it in the right way, the result is happiness. If we do anything in the right way, the result is happiness. The first book, of the series, is *Dance: A Spiritual Affair.* The second book is *Writing: A Spiritual Voice.* The third book is *Strange Words: Poems and Prayers.*

Part 1:

Nonfiction

Friend to All

Out of the Drawer

Like many people, I have always written. Like most people who write, I had no intention of being an author. I remember, as a young adult, a university friend telling me that my birthday and Christmas cards were so long that they were *like a book.* Later, in my mid-thirties, another friend told me, several times, that I could write a book about my life. I didn't think anything of that because everyone's life is interesting to themselves because they are the star.

People often feel that they have a book inside them. They probably do. However, the effort it takes to write, publish, and sell one is so demanding that few actually do it. If the writing voice is speaking to you, then, in some manner, you should listen. You do not have to become a published author, but all constructive inner drives are calling for action. The fulfilment of anything is in its expression. The joy is in the moment-by-moment attention, the developing ability to reach deeply into the creative centre, and the nurturing of an inherent individual impulse to create.

I began writing my first book, *The Love of Being Loving,* in 2005. I was in my mid-forties. The book came from decades of spiritual work, and lifetimes before that. It is a small book of 23,000 words, but it took me three years to write because I was a new writer and, true to my writing style ever since, I like to make every word count. After finishing it, I tried to get it accepted by a few publishing companies. As is generally the case, that went nowhere. In fact, I gave up after trying four publishing houses, which isn't many, but I felt I needed to go a different route. The manuscript sat in my desk drawer for another three years.

Life took a different turn and a long-term friendship turned into a couple relationship. As often happens with the introduction of new people into our life (or old people in a new way), it brought something fresh out of me. The dynamics of our own being and that of a totally other independent being fires up life. As my partner was a caring and intelligent man, also on the spiritual path, it was not perhaps a surprising outcome that I took the dormant book out of the drawer and got the momentum to self-publish it. The whole process of forming the idea, learning about self-publishing, and rewriting the book took another two years. The massive advances in self-publishing, which sprang from the ability to print-on-demand, were very timely for me. Finally, my book was published in 2013, having had an eight-year journey from inception to birth.

All authors know that the birth of a book is a huge milestone, but it also marks the beginning of the equally challenging journey to get it in front of people. That involves the making of oneself as a public persona with a particular voice. It involves marketing and selling. Otherwise, the manuscript might be out of the drawer and into the market, but it will be so invisible that it will not be doing much more than sitting in the drawer. The first of anything is the most difficult. Once that first book is written, edited (a million times if you edit yourself as I have always done), published, and some sort of marketing system is established, then books will have a much easier channel to flow through you.

My book became part of a four-book series, *Love and Devotion.* Another nonfiction series was also written – *The Creative Spirit Series* – which includes the gentle offering of a poetry book. Poetry is so private and personal. To my surprise, five years ago, after never having been a fiction reader, I started writing a fiction book, *Waldmeer,* which turned into a seven-book series.

Now, eight years after the release of my initial book, I have fourteen published books. The output was exponential, rather than being a steady production of books from the beginning. The last two years of COVID-19 have been a particularly valuable opportunity of concentrated time at home, and have seen the release of four nonfiction books and three fiction ones to finish the *Waldmeer Series*.

Needles and Haystacks

At the beginning of my writing career, my only goal was to get my book published with a publishing house. I knew nothing about self-publishing and had zero interest in it. I imagined, like most new authors, that if I could get a publishing house to take me, then I could do the part I liked (writing), and they could do everything else. The publishing industry has changed so much that virtually no one gets away with exclusively writing while someone else does everything else. Today, house-published or self-published, we are much more than people who only put pen to paper or fingers to computer. Authors could more accurately and broadly refer to themselves as *content creators*. We write books, but we also create all sorts of other content for all sorts of platforms.

When my book was published, I felt that I had made it; reached the goal, the end of the road, and now I could reap the rewards. Not quite knowing how exactly to get to those rewards, I decided to attend a writing workshop by the self-publishing company I had used for my book. Two things, from the workshop, made enough of an impression to stay in my mind.

The first was an author who had previously self-published with this company and whose book had done quite well. *Quite well* means that it had sold enough copies for the publishing house to take notice of it. She was consequently offered a book contract and was being held up as a model for us other self-publishers to aspire to. Obviously, I was interested to hear her speak. Her talk was uninspiring and later, when I bought her book to work out why it had sold and she had thus been offered a contract, I found it to be equally uninspiring.

The publishing house was a leader in the field of spiritual, self-development books, so my expectations had been set accordingly high.

This little story is not to disparage another author or that person's path or success. Good for her, in every way. It is, however, to say – go your own way, do your own thing, other people are not you. Publishing houses, whether *spiritual* or not, are businesses. They have to make money or they cannot survive. As a genuine, spiritually-driven writer, making money will not be your first goal. Of course, we need money to live, but if you are writing for spiritual purposes, then your number one goal will not be money. What makes a publishing house run does not particularly align with an author who is driven by spiritual motives.

After this one workshop, I never again aspired to be like another author or follow in their footsteps. That relatively new, mediocre author broke the spell of all other authors for me. It's like mothers. Outgrow your own mother and you will have outgrown the whole concept of seeking approval from people outside of yourself. Outgrow the publishing house of your dreams and you will have outgrown the whole concept of not being able to stand on your own feet as a writer.

If a publishing house contract works for you, then obviously go with that. Anyway, we should, at some stage, make an effort with the traditional publishing industry because it could be for us. However, if you have tried and gotten nowhere (which will be the case for the majority of writers), then disregard that path and form your own. For most writers, due to sheer logistics, it will not come their way.

In the fast-changing world of communication, do you even want to be involved with traditional publishing? Do you know that for every ten books a publishing house produces, seven will be a financial burden, two will break even, and one will hopefully make enough of a profit to support all the others? You certainly don't want to be the author losing money for your publisher, or the one breaking even. But do you want to be the one supporting everyone else? Maybe, maybe not.

Many people work in publishing because they would like to be successful writers themselves, but they can't make it work. This tells me that while they are capable of seeing what has been successful in the past, they cannot easily see what could be successful in the future. If they could, many of them would be writing it. Publishing houses sometimes complain that looking for new authors is like *looking for needles in haystack*s. I sometimes wonder if they are looking for the wrong needles in the wrong haystacks.

The world is changing, We can too. With today's technology, the world is accessible as never before, and it will only become more so at a rapid rate. Instead of begrudging that someone else doesn't consider us to be a needle worth searching for, we can build our own haystack and sit right at the top of it!

Author Platform

The second thing I remember from that writing workshop was a phrase I had not heard before, but I have since worked on every day. It was *author platform*. I listened carefully to what the professionals from the publishing house were saying about it. It was very basic but helpful information about writing a book being only half the battle. The other half was creating an author platform to reach someone; preferably, many someones. They explained that, as a self-published author, it was vital to do so. In the years since then, it has become necessary for every author, self-published or traditionally-published, to work on their overall platform and the many different arms that combine to make it.

As part of our author platform, we were told to have an active social media presence. Until that point, I had been anti-social media, as an individual. I wasn't on any social media, either personally or professionally. It seemed to me, all too often, that it was the domain of the superficial, competitive, boring, or lowest common denominator type of interaction. Nevertheless, that very evening, I reluctantly started a Facebook author page and, to my great surprise, it took off immediately. Since 2013, it has gained more than 350,000 followers from all over the world. That is a substantial following for an author.

Two years after starting my Facebook page, I did the same with YouTube and a similar thing happened. Again, I was reluctant to pursue it because of technical ignorance and also because I was nervous about putting myself in videos for the world to see. It seemed a very naked thing to do. There is a nakedness much more naked than an unclothed body. It is an unclothed soul. My YouTube channel gained almost 2 million views, and more than 50,000 hours of watch time, in the first few years alone.

Facebook and YouTube have been my biggest social media successes in terms of reach and numbers. However, I have tried everything and continue to try new things. I push myself to learn the new technologies because, just as I didn't know that Facebook and YouTube would work for me (in fact, I was sure they wouldn't), we never know what will prove a fortuitous avenue for us. I have not bothered to bore you with my many failures but, rest assured, they are endless. Some of my failures will be great successes for you.

Content Creators

As authors, along with our books, we write blogs, newsletters, and social media posts. We take and share photos, and we make videos. Many of us have learned to multi-task in our film-making endeavours and have been the starring actor, director, camera team, and makeup and costume department. We learn how to become content creators over a broad spectrum of mediums so that we can reach as many people as possible and engage with them in different ways. We have had to broaden our skills and have an open mind about all the forms of communication that are constantly expanding. Even if an author could get away with saying that they don't understand how to use social media, or work their phone camera, or edit a simple video, I think that they would be doing themselves a disservice by refusing to learn.

There is no reason why we cannot keep up with an evolving world. Learning is not the prerogative of the young. If you would like to keep an active and young mind, then it is best to exercise it. We mustn't denigrate the advances in technology because many people use them badly. We can use them well. There has never been a time in history when we can reach so many, so easily. We need to make technology work for us. It is a brilliant good fortune for our writing careers. In no other age have writers been able to make their own way in the writing world in such viable and effective ways without the machine of the publishing house. Grab the opportunities and work with them.

Unless we try to do a bit of everything, for our author platform, we will not know what we are good at and what works best for us. It may be very different to what we originally thought. Doors may be unexpectedly opened for us. In extending ourselves, we will be given a wider entrance into the world. To keep it all in perspective, it helps to remember that for all our content creating, there is one who is the master of content creation. The Divine is the true Creator and can inspire us with endless ideas for content and all other manner of creation.

Things I Don't Do

Some may say that I am not the best person to give writing advice. My academic education was not in literature and creative writing. It was in counselling. I had no ambitions as a writer. It never was a dream to be one. In one sense, it still isn't. Yet, I am one. In spite of my lack of formal education in the area of writing, and my lack of intention to be a writer, here, I happily am. I write not because I want to necessarily write. I write because it is a way of talking, and talking is a way of reaching people, and reaching people is a way of bringing more beauty, healing, and peace into the world. I am probably a missionary more than a writer; except that missionaries are denominational and I love all religions. I also love all people. As my primary concern has been people, not books, I have constantly made professional writing decisions based on whether or not they further my cause of people.

I am not particularly advocating my approach. I am not suggesting that you do what I do. Nor am I suggesting that you don't. Each writer must walk their own path. There are many different ways to write. Each is valid. Perhaps not valid for you, but valid for someone. What you should and shouldn't do will depend on many factors, such as experience, ability, talent, opportunity, intuition, inspiration, dedication, and one-minded focus.

My writing practices are not the norm. I don't do many of the things that are commonly recommended.

Things I Don't Do:

1. *Write every day.* Nearly all writing coaches say to write every day. I don't. I never have. I only write when I have something to say. Not something vague, but something very specific. Specific words, ideas, sentences. Because of this, unlike nearly all writers, I don't have excess writing. I don't have spare pages and books of ideas that have been played with and kept for later. My writing is based exclusively on what is told to me. Then, I edit it carefully. So, there is nothing left over, nothing spare, no previous copies of work, nothing lying around anywhere. I only write when I am *given* something to write, and I don't write any more than what I'm given. Who does the giving? The great Giver. What if I am given nothing? Then I write nothing. I don't consider it writer's block. That doesn't even cross my mind. I don't consider it anything. I just don't write.

2. *Practise writing.* The common advice is to sensibly practise. Of course, practice makes perfect or, more correctly, perfect practice makes perfect. However, does a young child practise talking? No, they just talk because of the drive to communicate and the need to express themselves. It's not a discipline. It's a drive. It's an inbuilt mechanism for survival, personal development, and expression. One only practises what is, in some sense, a chore or a duty. What is a

love, what is as natural as breathing, is not practised. It is simply done.

3. *Read.* They all say, and say many times, to read. I have never been a **fiction** reader although, these days, I write fiction as well as nonfiction. I'm still not a fiction reader. I simply don't read it. I do sometimes watch interesting movies or series to learn how they are structured. Even then, I don't spend hours watching them. I often watch the beginning and the ending, and then fast-forward through the rest, stopping instinctively at the important bits. Alternatively, I watch YouTube mash-ups which have compiled the best parts. It's very time efficient!

Although not a fiction reader, I was a very dedicated **nonfiction** reader of the spiritual books that interested me. The time-honoured wisdom of Buddha, Lao-Tzu, St. Francis of Assisi, Ramakrishna, and Meister Eckhart. The founding psychologists Freud, Jung, Maslow, and Erickson. The new thought of Mary Baker Eddy, Blavatsky, Rudolph Steiner, and Ernest Holmes. The inspiration of Kahlil Gibran, C.S. Lewis, and Edgar Cayce. The transpersonal psychology of Abraham Maslow, Carl Rogers, Ken Wilber, and Thomas Hora. The Bible, the Bhagavad Gita, A Course in Miracles, and other sacred texts. Now that I write my own nonfiction books, I no longer read them. Occasionally, I scan books to get the gist of them. That's it.

4. *Join writing groups.* Writers, almost universally, say to join them. I generally don't. I've joined life. That's enough of a group.

These are all intelligent recommendations and, although I don't do them, many, if not most, people will find them helpful in various ways. I don't do these things which are so sensibly recommended, but there is something I do do wholeheartedly. I listen. I listen, and then I write. My credentials for writing are no more than this. There is a voice that talks to me, and I listen to it and respond. And so, you shouldn't really take my advice except, of course, for one thing – you too want to listen to the inner voice. Then, we will listen together. And you will hear what is meant to come through you, and through your own writing.

Gardening Gods

"Isn't it the wrong time of year to prune roses?" said Kenny, my neighbour.

I was on a summer garden clean-up. My inner-city garden was small but, for twenty-five years previous, I had had a big suburban garden. I learned to garden very quickly and efficiently because of the time constraints of having young children and a large area to garden. Most of the time, my odd, personally-developed gardening methods worked.

"Should I be pruning mine too?" asked Kenny with the willingness of an eager apprentice.

He put his bin down and was surveying my garden closely as if to look for some magic, hidden recipe for success which he had somehow missed.

Kenny was a long-time househusband. He ran his house, organised his almost-grown children, and acted as a support person for his wife's busy career with ease. However, he was not quite so happy with his garden. Although respectable, he said it was lacking in comparison to other gardens he admired. His garden was tidy and manicured, but somewhat dreary. Organised, white, fashionably-common roses sat in a constrained row. A slab of grass only ever seemed to partially cooperate. A few strategically-placed pot plants broke up the monotony. The whole thing was adequate. Not inspiring. Kenny could be a little that way too. Lovely, decent, responsible, and intelligent but a little lacking pizzazz, spontaneity, thinking outside the box, and joy.

At one stage, the people in the property behind us built a high fence along their pathway. The pathway ran between my house and Kenny's house which meant that Kenny could no longer see my garden from his.

"Would you consider asking the back neighbours to lower the fence?" he had asked at one point. "I can't see your garden anymore, and I get a lot of pleasure from it."

The muddle of bright flowers and bulbs in my garden, the different heights of green, the buzz of bees, the mass of assorted roses of all colours and types somehow touched him. My little garden was the exact opposite of Kenny with all his success, privilege, and money (none of which he was ever pompous about). His house was four times the size of mine, and made mine look like a poor little cousin. With all that, he got enough pleasure from my humble garden to try and think up a way of seeing it easily again. Bless him.

At the time of the fence conversation, I explained that I quite liked the high fence because, although he had high fences all around his property, I was very open to passers-by, so I wanted to leave my one high fence. True to character, he totally understood.

Returning to the issue of pruning roses, Kenny asked again if he should also be pruning his.

"No, don't prune your roses," I said. "It's summer. It's hot. It's the wrong time of year." I then added by way of explanation about my untimely and severe mass pruning, "You know me, I garden by instinct. I want all the plants to get a second life in autumn. I'm trusting that they will cope with my heavy-handed cut-back."

Kenny told me, with great amusement, that one of our older Greek neighbours would get his chainsaw out to prune the roses and would spend five minutes wildly hacking off all the branches. Job done. I asked about the Greek neighbour's resulting roses.

"Beautiful," said Kenny with a half-disgusted laugh. "He had bloody beautiful roses."

He frowned as if to complain that the gardening gods were neither logical nor consistent. Kenny decided to go with the conventional schedule of rose-pruning (late winter), rather than my irregular one. We both knew that he would be watching my garden to decide upon the success or failure of the unconventional method.

Two weeks after speaking with Kenny about the untimely pruning, I glanced at my roses and noticed that, indeed, soft little shoots were bravely making their way through hardened, dead-looking wood. In no time at all, the bare wood would be covered with fresh life. Kenny will be sneaking peeks at it, telling himself that there must be a secret code of gardening that he is not privy to, and next time he will do whatever I do. That could, quite possibly, result in the death of his already underperforming, but beloved, roses.

Things I Do

Success in writing is similar to success in gardening.

Things I Do:

1. *Keep going.* Be patient. No one achieves anything without dedication and determination. If you are thrown by every negative, disappointing thing that happens, you won't get anywhere. The most successful people, in any field, have one-pointed focus. They do not get side-tracked, and they do not give up. Gardens take time and perseverance. So do writing careers. And everything else.

2. *Keep giving.* Don't stop planting. Whatever grows, then great. Whatever dies, take little notice. If you plant enough, then the things that die, or are stunted, pale into insignificance next to everything else which has flourished. Use failures and flops as learning devices. Keep moving forwards. Keep investing yourself, your money, your time, and everything else you have to offer. Trust your own destiny, but don't imagine that your destiny will destine on its own. Without you and your effort, your destiny won't lift a finger.

3. *Remain true.* Stay focused on what you personally love. Align with what you are naturally drawn to. I love cottage gardens; a mish-mash of colourful, simple joy. I love writing which inspires, challenges, and heals; accessible, direct, powerful messages

which everyone can understand, at some level. Believe in yourself and your own loves. Say what you have inside you. Say it bravely, and say it with good intent.

4. *Trust your instincts*. Write instinctively. To a certain extent, disregard what others think or do. Your instincts may be quite different to other people's.

5. *Go with the flow*. Don't be demanding and rigid about what the garden should look like. Go with the flow of the seasons and the garden's own life-force. Gardens change over time. They have a life-power of their own. Don't fight it. Join it, feed it, acknowledge it, respect it, and try to understand it. Neither be demanding and rigid about what your writing career should look like. Go with the flow of your writing path's own life-force. Don't fight it. Join it, feed it, acknowledge it, respect it, and try to understand it. Work with it. Work as a team with all the forces which are there to help you.

6. *Do your best.* The effort you put in will be rewarded. Sometimes, your best will be better than at other times. Do your best, one day at a time. That's good enough. Your writing path will grow beautifully. You don't know who may get value from something you have said or done. More people than you realise can be blessed by something you do. It spreads out like a ripple in a pond. We only get told a small fraction of the effect we have on other people. When we get the occasional compliment, we can take it as a reminder

that there are people out there benefiting from what we are doing.

7. *Enjoy it.* Take pleasure from what you have helped to create. Enjoy your writing as you would your garden. It's never finished. It's ongoing. So, relax and enjoy the beauty and life which is in it today, right where it is. Although our everything has to go into creating our writing career, we cannot claim it as our own. Our career is no more ours than our garden. If we would like it to flourish, it is wise to humbly remember that we work with God. Our boss is the best, and will not forget our loyalty and dedication. In fact, we will get far more from our Boss then we will ever have to give.

Books and Babies

In 2014, a small book launch of my second book, *The Love of Devotion*, was organised by a mother at my children's school. Mothers are mighty creatures of the world. *The hand that rocks the cradle* (and parents the teenager) *rules the world.* For several weeks after the book launch, one Mum was, rather endearingly, carrying around, in her handbag, her wrapped copy of *The Love of Devotion* which had been given to her at the launch. She wasn't ready to read it, but nor did she want to take it out of her bag.

Her husband, who was an avid reader, decided that he wanted to read the book and kept asking her for it. Somehow, she never quite got to giving it to him. Without her knowing, he took matters into his own hands. When she wasn't looking, he got the book out of her bag, took it out of the paper wrapping, replaced it with another book, wrapped it up again, and put it back in his wife's handbag. He happily and secretly read my book.

Sometime later, his wife decided that she was now ready to read the book and took it out of her handbag. She unwrapped it and then couldn't understand why I had given her a book about baby names instead of *The Love of Devotion*. They were definitely past baby days. Her husband enjoyed the joke so much that he was reluctant to explain the confused identity of the stolen book.

Woman in White

A few days before the photo shoot for the book cover of *The Love of Devotion,* I suddenly had the idea to wear a large, white, silk veil over my body and head. I have used the resulting image as my author photo, on the back cover of this book, so that you can see it.

The veil is a universal representation of feminine spiritual devotion. It is ancient and transcultural. It represents the core qualities of spiritual love and inner beauty. It has its own particular manifestations in each religion, but is always equated with humility before God, devotion to goodness, and commitment to the spiritual path. My natural self is highly devotional. As a Westerner, and a raised Catholic, the archetypal symbol was probably arising from the stereotypic Catholic nun.

At the time, I didn't ask anyone's opinion about my veil-wearing idea because I knew everyone would say not to do it. The veiled image of a female author is hardly a spiritually-fashionable, upbeat, or comfortable concept in the Western world. Even the Catholic nuns have abandoned the veil. The Western world has been engrossed in its scientific and psychological explorations for a long time. It has been far too busy for the supposedly old-fashioned concept of spiritual devotion. Nevertheless, Spirit told me to wear it, so I did.

At that stage of my career, I had my author eyes on the Western world only. That world was, not surprisingly, disinterested in my veiled image of devotion. However, to my total surprise, the rest of the world loved it. It hadn't crossed my mind that other places, different to my place-of-birth, would be interested in me. I uploaded the image of my white-veiled, blue-eyed, blonde-haired devotional self on my newly-formed Facebook author page. That one photo significantly contributed to my Facebook page taking off. The Christians, in places other than the West, loved it. The Muslims, everywhere, loved it. The Hindus loved it.

I had no idea what I was doing, or who was supporting my new page, or why exactly. I was suddenly virtual-travelling in a great range of countries that I knew nothing about. I wondered if it was an accident, or fluke, or if they would unfollow me if they realised that I wasn't *one of them.*

I explained the situation to a few professionally-accomplished authors and marketers, and asked for their opinion as to why it was happening and what to do about it. One said it was just the photo and it would all die off soon. Another said that I had done everything the wrong way and that, if I wanted my presence to be sustainable, I needed to follow his advice. Another, more-developed soul, said that he didn't know why it was happening, but wished me well and said to keep going.

Eventually, after going from strength to strength, it dawned on me that, maybe, it wasn't a mistake. Maybe, the people did know what they were doing or, at least, they knew one thing. They could tell who I was. They recognised devotion. Devotion is gravely missing in the West, but it is not missing in many other parts of the world. The better we think we are doing, the less we tend to talk to the Divine. My followers and supporters recognized my spiritual integrity and goodwill, and were not afraid to align with it and show their appreciation. The veil is humility before God, Allah, Brahman, and all the names that the Divine answers to. Humility is recognition of the spiritual dimension to empower, transform, heal, and guide us.

Gaining Trust

One of the first countries to enthusiastically follow my Facebook author page was Afghanistan. I was told (by them) that, initially, they thought I was Muslim (because of the veil). Little did they know that, at that stage, I barely knew any Muslims and, although I was open to all religions, I knew almost nothing about Islam. As you know, in regards my veil, I was thinking Catholic nun. Possibly, a dash of Hindu woman – a theatrical cross between Bollywood and Shakti, the Supreme Spirit.

In the first few years, I gained 25,000 followers from Kabul alone. They were nearly all young men. That's a veritable army of young men wanting to move forward to a better world. The young men of our world have a great deal of power to change it by the way they educate themselves, dedicate themselves to their work, love their women and children, and develop their inner being so that it is as marvellous as they can make it. The Afghans are still strong followers in spite of the recent withdrawal of the U.S. forces.

During those initial years of Afghan interest, a high-ranking U.S. military personnel, who was stationed in Afghanistan, wrote to me and said, "I must say you have a wonderful profile here and you are sterling. I saw your profile and it warmed my heart. The impact has been overwhelming, and we are so interested in what you are doing."

In a later correspondence, he said, "You have been able to do what we have not. The Afghans tolerate us, but we have never been able to gain their trust."

27

There are many things an army can do and, unfortunately, they are still necessary. However, what billions of U.S. defence dollars cannot do, we *can* do by reaching out with love, respect, and hope.

The warrior archetype is embedded in the Afghan culture. They highly value their ability to protect their families, traditions, and country. In such a climate, it was not surprising that they were reluctant to give their trust to an outside military presence, although they needed them for stability. What they lacked in trust towards foreign men, they did not lack towards the outstretched hand of feminine love which carried no weapon and no ulterior motive. If men, and in particular young men, have a fire inside for peace and life-improvement, they cannot be pulled into the fire that burns with hate, despair, and ignorance.

My virtual-presence in Afghanistan seemed to give the U.S. military officer a sense of hope that, when the time came to leave, the many problems they would be leaving behind might have a chance of being managed in a more viable way. That day of the U.S. leaving has recently arrived. Afghanistan is far from managing its problems in a viable way. Nevertheless, the world is getting smaller and we are all getting closer. That helps with the movement towards a more unified and peaceful mankind and womankind.

I feel my devotional message is as much needed, if not more, in the West. What we have in wealth and scientific /medical /educational advances, we have, in large part, lost in our spirit. That spirit is more alive in the non-Western world. The West must learn to reconnect with its soul. We have a lot to give each other. We are unequivocally valued in the sight of God as men, women, and children – every culture, every skin colour, every demographic, rich and poor, every individual preference. That is the starting point. Not the endpoint. The beginning of creating a harmonious and flourishing world is to start from the basis of equal value. One world. One people. Different expressions. All loved. All valued.

Friend to All

We are in this together. In what? Life. As a spiritual being, we see everyone as a friend. And when we write, we write to our friends; everyone. Love is unifying, not dividing. It speaks its own language. That language is always uniting.

People are, in essence, the same. They want to be happy. They enjoy love stories and find them inspiring. Men will defend women and children with their lives. Women will do whatever it takes to nurture and protect their families. People want a better life. They want to learn and be educated. I am inspired by the great, common driving force – the desire for love, in every form. Love gives life meaning in a way nothing else can. If we focus on the inner world which makes us all the same, then the outer world will not seem in such conflict. It will be enlivening not dividing, enriching not impoverishing, uniting not damaging.

Giving Away to Keep

When we are transforming ourselves, on the spiritual path, we automatically want to help others to do the same as it strengthens and accelerates our own transformation. Whatever we would like to make stronger in ourselves is strengthened by sharing it with others. When we share, we gain. When we withhold, we lose. When we give away, we keep. Wherever we are with our growth, we should share that with the world in ways that are natural and enjoyable to us. Everything we share is made stronger in our own being.

In every situation in which we find ourselves, we should keep our thoughts on contributing to and improving the environment. What can I give to this person, group, situation? We mustn't focus on trying to get people to give us what we want. We must focus on turning ourself into a more loving being who is using as much of their potential as possible to reach out to a world full of friends.

Nonpersonal Persona

Our marketing needs to be honest, service-oriented, and spiritually aligned. To make our work available to as many people as possible, we need to tell them about it. Marketing is letting people know that we exist. For some people, it is best to make their marketing about their books. For others, it will need to be about the author – you. Don't take it personally, even if it's you.

A large part of my marketing is about me because that's what works. It may mean a lot of selfies and other personal sharing, but I don't view it as personal. People need something that they can relate to. They often need an actual person to connect to in order to connect with that person's work. They need a face, and more. It's not egoically personal. Nor is it fake. It needs to be authentic and generous so that people become interested enough in us and our work that they will want to listen, read, and follow. My author persona is carefully crafted, but it is still very much me. In fact, I get to express the best of me without having to modify my communication as I often have to in ordinary life. I can focus entirely on what I think is best for people to know. If they don't like it, they don't have to read or watch it.

Understanding the nonpersonal nature of the author persona gives us protection from both criticism and adoration. If people criticise us for being egocentric or unspiritual, we know that we are being neither, but simply meeting needs in the most effective way. If they criticise our work, what does it matter? If we receive love and adoration, what does it matter? When we feel loved by life, neither criticism nor praise changes our sense of security and well-being. We know that the purpose of our work is to help others. How people feel about us is not the point. Our focus is on sharing the Divine presence so that others can benefit. We are a medium and channel, not an end in itself.

Any God-given gift we have been blessed with is public property in the sense that we have been given it for the good of all. This saves us from many an ego-trip. It guarantees the purity of the gift. It ensures the success of our endeavours.

Selling and Sharing

Selling is sharing. We are sharing our gift. We are sharing information and knowledge. We are sharing ourself. First, we must make sure that our product is the best that it can be. That takes years of absolute commitment. Then, we must turn our mind to discovering the best ways we can reach people with our offering. Share what you have from the basis of love, not from the basis of bargaining, or you will be greatly watering down your capacity to flourish. Share your work because you want to share. Show by your consistent actions that you are interested in sharing for the benefit of others' well-being.

For us, in Melbourne, Australia, the bulk of the last two years has been some version of lockdown due to the pandemic. One of my main isolation tasks has been to try and master the massive machine of Amazon ads. As my books are predominantly on Amazon, it is an obvious place for me to advertise. It will differ for each author, and there is a great deal to learn in any of the marketing avenues which we may choose to explore. Never stop learning or believing that what you have to give is worth the effort to learn how to give it in the most effective manner. If we aren't willing to try things and learn about the relevant processes which could help us, then people aren't going to find what we have to share with them.

Presence Not Pity

It's not easy to make your author presence work well on social media. In an attempt to bring it to life, some authors turn their personal social media into a platform for their public author work. They constantly barrage their friends with information about their books and requests for support. It is often phrased in such ways as, "Let's support each other," or "Help me make my dream come true." The person may indeed get a response, but much of it is some version of pity. Don't pester your friends on social media for support of your author work. If you are asking for support from your friends (no matter how you phrase it), then you are not in a position to be giving them anything. They are giving you something – pity, kindness, positivity, money (as in buying books), emotional support.

It is better to have two genuine followers of your work on any public platform than five hundred friends who feel sorry for you. If all you honestly have to give, at this stage, is appreciated by only a few independent followers, then accept that, be grateful, and grow yourself in any and every way you can think of. A public social media presence is just that. It's public. It has to stand on its own merits. It is not asking for help or support. It is giving something. If the public feel that what is being given is something that they want, then they will start to pay attention. If we would like people to follow us on social media, read our books, watch our videos, and be interested in what we are offering, we must be devoted. Devoted to what? Them; not our own career. Their well-being; not our own success.

35

Don't be the judge and jury of your own work. Do your best to perfect each aspect of it, and then get it out into the world. Let the world, be it ten people or ten million, tell you how helpful it is and in what ways. That will be valuable fodder for your future growth as an author. We, as individuals, are not really capable of seeing ourselves objectively. We need others to be a mirror for us. Keep planting. Let the passers-by tell you how lovely your garden is.

Competition

Be careful of your peers. They can sometimes be harmless, sometimes even helpful. They can also be deadly. If you are intending to do well in your chosen career, I would be careful about spending too much time with peers who are struggling. Writers, like all artists, put enormous effort into their work for generally little in return. The ego, no matter how sweetly it dresses itself, cannot help but feel that one person's success is an opportunity taken away from itself in an intensely competitive market. Don't fall prey to it. Also, make sure that you are not one of those author-egos, yourself.

Healthy competition is not detrimental to our well-being and progress. It is advantageous. It highlights the skills that others have. It's a teaching and motivating device. It helps us to see the weaker areas within ourselves that need improvement. Other people's strengths are not disadvantageous to us. They can inspire and push us to develop those same elements within our own being. Turn the flame of jealousy into the fire of self-improvement.

As a rule, don't compare yourself to other writers. Give what you are authentically capable of giving. It is not a competition. It is a love. Is a mother capable of loving all her children? So too is Life capable of loving all of us, as different as we are.

Friends and Bitches

Write like God is your best friend, but edit like a tough bitch. Or, as the saying goes, *Write drunk, edit sober.*

People drink to escape the pain of life and to escape the boundaries of themselves. The idea of writing *drunk* is to write bravely and without boundaries. As spiritual writers, we don't need outside chemistry to be happy and creative. We learn how to be intoxicated with the beauty of life and the love of the Divine. That is an endless source of inspiration, freshness, and intelligence. Write as if God is talking directly to you; not just talking like an acquaintance, but talking intimately like a lover. When God is your best friend, you don't need to escape anything. You don't need pain relief because you are not in pain. You don't need to escape the drudgery of life because life is a joy and way too short. Life is only long when we are unhappy.

When I write, the writing first forms in my soul. I will suddenly get an idea or a sentence, when I am not thinking about it. Often, I get an idea in my sleep. It is an intuitive and unforced process. However, after the flow of inspiration, there needs to also be a rational and intellectual process. We must edit, and re-edit, with patience and precision. My ex-partner will tell you that I am a tough editor. He would steel himself to give me something he had written. The response would be some version of this.

"You have six different ideas here instead of sticking to one. It doesn't flow. It jumps from one thought to another without any connection. Do you really know what you are saying experientially? It is preachy. It's boring. It's too long. Be succinct. It's playing safe. Be more transparent. Be braver. You are not giving enough of yourself."

Out of a whole page of writing, he would end up with a few sentences left. And he was a good writer and excellent public speaker. No, my tough editing is not why he is an ex.

Make It Count

My style, as a writer, is succinct. I don't write empty words for the sake of filling a page. Writers often talk about word-count as if it is a valuable thing in and of itself. I understand the intention of high quantity writing output. I know that writers who write for income have to have quantity. However, I think in terms of quality; spiritual quality. To have spiritual quality means that our work must carry the power to heal and transform. Write the right words; not a lot of words. For every word that you ask your readers to read, they are giving you the gift of their attention. Make it count.

In poetry, particularly, every word counts. Counts for what? In mystical poetry, it counts for beauty, connection, insight, encouragement, and inspiration. It counts if it opens a door, opens a heart, opens a space. The challenge of poetry is to convey meaning in very few words. It is to share a message with only the hint of language. In order to communicate through poetry, we must reach directly and deeply into an issue, person, or situation. We must grab onto the core of something and present it to the reader so that they can't look away.

Read Your Own Books

Our primary role, as spiritual writers, is not to entertain or educate, although we do both. Our primary role is to provide spiritual help which becomes a manifest and visible reality in the individual reader's life. If no change happens, then either we did not do our job or they did not do theirs.

However, before we get to assisting others, the very first person our writing should be valuable to is ourselves. Why wouldn't it be? If what we write can't help us, then it will have little chance of helping anyone else. It is only conceited to think about our own writing in this way if we think we invented it. But if we are writing via the Divine inner voice, then wouldn't we want to listen to that voice too?

After looking at something you have created, ask yourself if you, personally, benefited from hearing /writing /reading it. I regularly read my own books because the Divine spirit gave me the words and ideas. How ungrateful it would be to not make the most of something that someone (immensely superior) graciously gave me. It is meant for me, as much as it is meant for anyone else.

If you don't think that what you write is good enough to help you and hold your interest, then make something else that corresponds to your highest sense of what you are capable of creating. You are very blessed to have the gift of writing. You are even more blessed to have the gift of being able to hear the Inner Voice.

Don't Waste Time

When we understand the fragility of life, we live consciously. People generally live as if they have all the time in the world. They don't. They have the time of one lifetime, however long that will be. It's not a lot.

We don't have enough time for procrastinating and wasting large chucks of our life. When we give our attention and love to anything in life, it is a valuable offering. What we spend our time on will determine the course of our life. If we know that we are here for a short time, our choices will become more meaningful and satisfying. We don't have to be told to be brave and follow our inner leanings when we are aware of our limited time. Who cares what other people think of us when we are busy living a brief life to the best of our ability? We will want to use every day to better ourselves and the world we live in.

We mustn't turn our back on opportunity. For those who take up what life offers, there seem to be gifts and open doors everywhere. The doors that are closed and the gifts that are withdrawn pale into insignificance compared to the throbbing mass of life-opportunities which abound.

Expression of Life

It is encouraging to feel that if we listen to the inner voice, we will be led. Everyone has a purpose, and fulfilling our purpose will make us happy. Whatever our individual purpose is, it will always be to use our abilities to add something good to other people's lives and thereby add to own.

Creativity, in any form, is a high-level expression of Life. There should be an element of surprise in our creative expressions; both to us and others. What is created should move us with its newness and freshness. Yet, it will also seem as old as life, and just as sure.

Trust the creative process. Trust the artistic process of writing. Trust the process of your life. Remember, you are the greatest work of art yourself. Don't hold back from life's challenges for fear of failure or you will miss out on life, itself. You are a walking, breathing, writing mass of possibilities and potential.

Part 2:

Fiction

Friends with Different Names

Something Lovely

About five years ago, a handyman was fixing my dishwasher. He had recently returned from some work in Byron Bay.

"There's a lot of work up there," he said.

Byron Bay is made up of backpackers, surfers, hippies, hipsters, and generally *woke* people. There are probably more Reiki practitioners than any other profession. The tourists save the economy. The sign at the town entrance says,

> *Welcome to Byron Bay.*
> *Cheer Up. Slow down. Chill out.*

"Yes," I laughed. "Too many yogis and not enough practical people to repair stuff."

On leaving my house, out of the blue, he asked me what sort of work I did.

"I'm a writer," I replied.

At that point, I had published my third nonfiction book, *Love's Longing*, a few months previous and hadn't written anything since. As I only write when directed, and there had been no direction, nothing had been written. Even the desire to write seemed to have left me.

For no apparent reason, he said earnestly, "You are a sweet woman. Write something lovely for the world."

He was quite a bloke and the comment seemed uncharacteristic. I wondered if the esoteric culture of Byron Bay had affected him. Then, I thought no more about his comment which I relegated to *cute, not important*. However, as if his words had the power of creation, I started writing again that very evening. My repair man was an unintentional messenger. He was announcing an arrival.

What I wrote was, very surprisingly, fiction; a short story about pain, healing, and jealousy. I did not know that it was the first chapter of a book. I certainly had no idea that it would be the first book of a long series. Nevertheless, it was the beginning of my fiction writing path. As explained previously, I had never written, or even considered writing, fiction. I was not a fiction reader, except for teenage years spent reading Mills and Boon romance curled up on the bed, with my cousin, in school holidays. As my repairman-messenger had said, *Something lovely for the world,* had begun.

Delightful, Intriguing, Comforting

Recently, a reader of the *Waldmeer Series* said, "I'm so enjoying your energy and voice via the *Waldmeer Series* books. I find it delightful, intriguing, and comforting." The reader chose her words instinctively, and they accurately describe the series.

1. *Delightful* – Waldmeer is an idyllic coastal village with stunning natural beauty. It is a place of healing with its quiet, repetitive rhythm and has remained relatively undamaged by the outside world. The simple events of Waldmeer belie the far more complex events of the interdimensional worlds. I wanted to use the delightful home base of Waldmeer to give a backdrop of reassurance while the reader progressed through the struggles of both this world and the other dimensions. Eventually, the reader would get the sense that a place like Waldmeer can be made, by themselves, wherever they go because they can be *at home* anywhere in the world. On finishing *Waldmeer (Book 1),* a friend said wistfully, "I want to live in Waldmeer and I want to be Amira." Amira is our collective spiritual self. Her intentions are good, mistakes are easily corrected, and pride is not an issue. We are all drawn to our truest selves, and we want to live in safety, peace, and happiness.

2. *Intriguing* – The most intriguing thing in life is people and the way they relate to each other; the depths they will go to and the heights; the intensely fascinating way that people and their relationships evolve. The strongest, most attractive, most engaging element of life is relationships and the crazy, beautiful forms they take. They are intrinsically intriguing. Although my prime goal in writing the *Waldmeer Series* has been the spiritual evolution of individuals, individual people learn best in the context of their relationships. Relationships are our most potent learning form. The spiritual path is very practical and relevant. This is particularly so in our personal relationships which have more power to change us than anything else. The purpose of the series is not merely to entertain. It is to challenge, help, and inspire. Honest problems. Honest growth. Without intrigue, the journey would be abandoned before the lessons were given a chance.

3. *Comforting* – The series is ultimately comforting because spiritual truth is comforting. Most people are deeply uncomfortable in life. If they allow themselves to be led along the spiritual path, they will certainly find comfort and freedom. More than an engaging story, the *Waldmeer Series* is a doorway to personal and spiritual growth. Our potential, in every way, is far greater than we understand. Spiritual reality is always pushing us towards evolution, healing, love, and freedom.

It's a Given

Right from the beginning, the *Waldmeer Series* has been written, chapter by chapter, as I have been given the material to write. Once written, it has been posted on my website as a blog. It is unusual to write a novel (more so, a series) as an ongoing blog. Normally, books are written and rewritten, many times, before even a page is published. Although I carefully edit each blog post before it is public, once it is posted, it remains unchanged. That means that there are around 200,000 words which have essentially not been altered since they have been posted (except for the occasional word and some grammatical editing).

I have only been a week or so ahead of readers in knowing what will happen in the plot and so I am always interested to see which characters appear and what happens to them. I find it funny when I am told amusing things that will happen or that characters will say, especially ridiculous things. I find it sad when they refuse to grow. I find it wonderful and satisfying when healing and love happen.

I am often surprised and delighted how things work out so beautifully and connectedly in the long run. As I don't know where the story is going, there are many examples of later finding out why it was necessary for certain things to happen in a particular way. Even the character's names are very specifically given. They don't get a name until I'm sure it's the right one. One example is Maria /Amira's name. I was given Amira as a name first, as she appeared earlier in the book, in spirit form. I knew her name meant *one who speaks* which seemed appropriate. Later, I needed a human name for Amira's Earth-counterpart. The inner voice told me, Maria. I thought it was sweet because my childhood friend was Maria. It was only after a week or so that I realised Amira and Maria were the same letters, in different order, and I thought how clever the guides are.

Sometimes, a very minor character is introduced. Good writers know that it is detrimental to bring in characters who add no real value. At the time, I might wonder why a certain person or scene has surfaced, for no apparent reason, and hope that eventually that person /place will have a purpose. Without fail, they do. Readers often need to hear of someone or something a long time before that person or place has a significant value to the story. So, being planted, earlier on, is important. It requires confidence in the listening-writing process. These types of little things (and sometimes big things) have happened repeatedly. In fact, too many times to recall, but it has given me great trust that those who give me the story know exactly what they are doing.

Many parts of the *Waldmeer Series* have come from dreams, for example, *Circles of Separation (Book 3): Outer Circle*. The interdimensional Outer Circle problem of forgetting who one really was and why one was there, the ticket collector scammers and scanners (the scanners scanning tickets with their thumbs and the way the lines rearranged to give them information about the person), the menacing Dream Maker who could do nothing without one's consent – they all came from a dream. Try to remember your dreams. They are a valuable source of information, creativity, and discovery.

Sometimes, when a section is finished, a thought pops into my mind, *That's the best thing I've ever read.* Obviously, I do not really think that it is the best thing that has ever been written. However, I think it is the angel's way of telling me,

It's done. Then, I can leave the section in peace. That is, until they start talking again.

Nonnegotiable - Fair

There are several essential elements of the writing process which I know are nonnegotiable from the Ones who tell me the story. How I relay the story and its meaning must be done in a particular way. It must be fair. It must be real. It must be simple.

The story and its process must be fair in the sense that everyone will be treated in the same way. It is based on the principle that all characters, being people, are seen as equally valued by God. This does not negate their faults and failures, but it does mean that no one can be abandoned as less deserving than anyone else. It is definitely not allowed for me to make something bad happen to someone I don't like or something good happen to someone I want to protect. For this reason, I am careful about letting my children transmute into characters.

Fair means equally entitled. Everyone is equally entitled to their spiritual heritage. All characters are seen as worthy of value. God does not have favourites. No one is regarded as unworthy of every opportunity to change their minds, regardless of how many times they have turned their backs on those opportunities previously. Certainly, no one must be hated. Characters will sometimes bring out hateful feelings from other characters and from readers, and quite rightly. Some things are woeful. That is part of the story-telling medium.

However, the general overriding viewpoint, or the point of view of the narrator, is from the highest perspective. It does not have the luxury of seeing characters in a flawed, limited, human way. The question must be asked, *How would a parent feel about this person?* If a human parent can love their wayward offspring, God certainly can.

To see people in this way is to have a highly developed sense of compassion for human suffering. It is to realise that no one is suffering on purpose. We give up the pleasure we feel in self-righteously blaming others. Healing has a chance when we see people without blame.

On finishing reading *Waldmeer (Book 1),* my sister said, "There is a little bit of each character in all of us." I thought that was a succinct and humble observation as she was including the good, bad, easily-loved, ugly, adorable, and challenged characters and stages they go through.

As a writer, we need to see people and characters very clearly for what they humanly are. We must see faults more astutely, accurately, and painfully than normal people do. Otherwise, our writing will come across as unbelievable, insincere, irrelevant, or boring. However, as a spiritual writer, we do not blame people and characters for what they cannot yet understand.

Nonnegotiable - Real

On a drive to quaint country town, Daylesford, I went into a rustic bookshop with rows and rows of old books in peculiar little off-shoot rooms. The books looked like they were long-time loved and admired by their master and shop owner. He had collected an astounding amount of beautiful, bygone books over many years.

I picked up a used copy of a children's book which was published one hundred years ago. It was a moving, ageless story for children and their adult readers alike; a book that I read to my children when they were young. Books like it go into the back recesses of one's consciousness and help form the collective unconscious.

It was *The Velveteen Rabbit* (or *How Toys Become Real*) and was written for anyone who has ever wondered if becoming real hurts and if it is worth it.

> "Real isn't how you are made," said the Skin Horse. "It's a thing that happens to you. When a child loves you for a long, long time, not just to play with, but REALLY loves you, then you become Real."

> "Does it hurt?" asked the Rabbit.

> "Sometimes," said the Skin Horse, for he was always truthful. "When you are Real you don't mind being hurt."

"Does it happen all at once, like being wound up," he asked, "or bit by bit?"

"It doesn't happen all at once," said the Skin Horse. "You become. It takes a long time. That's why it doesn't happen often to people who break easily, or have sharp edges, or who have to be carefully kept. Generally, by the time you are Real, most of your hair has been loved off, and your eyes drop out and you get loose in the joints and very shabby. But these things don't matter at all, because once you are Real you can't be ugly, except to people who don't understand."

***

The second nonnegotiable principle of my writing process is that I must relay the story and its meaning in a way that is real. All characters must face their issues honestly. Just like life. There is no escaping. Nothing can be candy coated or skipped for convenience. All progress, or lack of it, must be realistic in terms of the sorts of things that different types of people think and do.

The path to healing looks a particular way for different kinds of folk. Angry people don't suddenly become calm. They have to learn how to acknowledge and process their rage. Fearful people don't magically become brave. They have to have an experience of being put in a situation that is so unacceptable (usually because they, or someone they love, is hurt in an unacceptable way) that they make the giant leap to courage. Sad people don't miraculously become happy. They must understand the unconscious ways that they continuously choose unhappiness as a state of consciousness. By understanding this, they can slowly learn to rechannel their thoughts into more life-enhancing and healthy mindsets.

No character escapes, in the long run, going through this rather gruelling but beneficial process. My ex-partner once said, "No one in *Waldmeer* is safe." He meant that every character would have to meet his or her Maker in terms of their underlying thoughts and intentions. While it is true that no one gets to hide, it is also true that there is no need to hide. The intention of both myself and the guides is to help and heal, not harm.

In life, my natural preference for communication has a depth of *realness* which most people find uncomfortable or confronting. To me, being real is normal. Being pretentious, dishonest, superficial, manipulative, or delusional is not on the register.

A little while back, my daughter laughed at something I said to another person. After I explained why I didn't think it was unusual to say it, she said, *That's why it's funny. You think it's normal. It's not.* She was probably implying that it might be prudent to be a bit more normal on some occasions. However, I think,

1. *Why not say the truth because it is obvious* anyway? I can see through people, and so can most others even if they are not aware of it. People tend to wrongly think that their inner being is invisible; that they are doing a good job of hiding it and should continue with that line of attack.

2. *We are all made of the same stuff,* with different combination of elements, so there is nothing that needs hiding.

3. Life is too short not to make progress, and *without honesty there is no change.* We don't make progress without honest confrontation of that which needs changing.

4. *Life would be terribly boring if I didn't communicate deeply.* Normally, I am silent (or close to silent) in social situations which I deem as worthless. I'm not incapable of socialising skilfully. I can socialise like the best of them. Generally, however, I choose not to. It is not shyness or unmanaged introversion. It is a deliberate decision to not invest energy into situations lacking realness.

Nonnegotiable - Simple

Apart from being fair and real, the guides also instruct that the story and its lessons must be simple. Sometimes, the guides explain to me a complex spiritual idea in sophisticated words. Then they say, *Put that in the book simply*. Not an easy task. Only when something is truly understood can it be explained simply. Fortunately, they do not leave me alone in the task. They give me both the ideas of the story and often the specific words and phrases to use.

In particular, the story needs to start simple. The beginning of a story has to lure in the reader because they don't yet know and love the characters. They don't want an overload of detail, introspection, or depth. The characters evolve with time and life-experience. Initially, we have to be polite enough to not bombard our dear readers with too much information and insight. It's quite a trick to give our characters all the essential elements of their nature, but not to tire the reader. The start of a book or series is the tentative, hopeful, gurgling creek which will end up as a mighty river drawing everything, in its path, towards the endless sea from which one does not return.

Language

My first two nonfiction books (*Love and Devotion* Series) use specific metaphysical language because that's how I learned the ideas that are being explained. The language of those spiritual traditions served me well in my evolution. The relevant teachers used erudite, sophisticated language; metaphysical, psychological, philosophical, and often unique to particular traditions. I understood the teachers because I knew those languages. However, I wanted people, not familiar with that type of language, to understand the teaching too. So, I tried to explain the ideas in more common, accessible language without losing the power of the teachings.

The Love of Being Loving (my first nonfiction book) is based on the teachings of Dr Hora. When I was a brand-new student of his, at the age of twenty-two, one of my questions to him, in my phone counselling session from Australia to New York, was, "Dr Hora, why do you use such big words?" Words such as phenomenology and existentialism were rife. I understood the words because I read a lot, but I didn't see the purpose of using them and making life complicated for the spiritual seeker.

Dr Hora repeated my question, a little surprised, to make sure he understood my accent, and said, "Are they big? It's because we need people to understand the exact meaning of these ideas. We don't use big words for the sake of it, but they have very particular meanings. If the students learn to understand what the words mean, they will be better able to understand the concepts."

Essence of the Lesson

Writing fiction, as compared to nonfiction, has been a whole other level of making things simple in order for the message to be accessible. One of the main points of writing fiction, for me, has been to reach those who don't read nonfiction and so aren't availing themselves of the opportunity to learn the concepts of spiritual development. I sometimes think, with a little amusement, that writing fiction is a long, drawn-out, convoluted way of writing nonfiction. It takes much longer, more scene setting and conversations, and more jollying along to get to the same point, but the point *is* the point.

The whole dynamic of storytelling is to set the scene for something important to occur which is generally encapsulated in the words of characters, at strategic points, along the way. When we recall loved novels, we recall moments of meaning, change, and insight. Often, we can remember the exact words that were said. Like in life, whatever words are planted in the back of our minds, as memories, have the power to change us.

Good fiction is not only based on believable and interesting characters but, at its centre, is *the quote*. Quotes are the essence of the lesson.

Therapy

Story-telling is a wonderful outlet for expressing all sorts of emotions and thoughts. It's very therapeutic. I once listened to an author who said, "I feel sorry for people who don't write because what do they do with all the stuff that happens to them?"

When I first started writing fiction, I told my son what a great outlet writing fiction was compared to writing nonfiction. I said, "All the things that have ever happened to me, but I wasn't able to deal with properly (because of age, emotional inability, or the situation didn't allow it), I now get to express with as much rage, indignation, hurt, passion, grief, or deep love as I want. I love it!"

Stories are therapeutic for writer and reader alike. Recently, my friend, and a reader of the series, said, "You are too confronting." He shook his head as if to say, *I can't deal...*

I couldn't help laughing. He is relatively equipped to deal with my therapeutic confrontation. I replied, "Isn't it good if it makes your life better?"

He walked off.

I thought, *Obviously, not.*

My friend wasn't saying that I was wrong. Nor was he saying that it wasn't for his own good. He was saying that it was hard. Too hard. I know it's hard, but suffering from stupidity and ignorance is worse.

We have to choose our people and the right moment to address issues head-on, both in life and story-telling. I choose to be confronting when I think it has a chance. That isn't terribly often in real life. People don't cope. It is, however, much more frequent in my fiction. If readers can't cope with it, then they can put the book down and walk away. Just like my friend did.

Endings and Bookends

Endings are as important as beginnings. They need a lot of thought; the exact right idea from the exact right source. I particularly love the ending of *Faith (Book 4)* which centres on a poem.

> *The last useless battle,*
> *someone with fall.*
> *Useless but useful,*
> *for nothing, for All.*

I feel the ending encapsulates the whole human journey – the struggle to find peace within ourselves and each other. All the struggle disappears in those moments of acceptance, trust, and love. It disappears into nothingness as if it was all totally unnecessary. Yet, without the struggle, we could not have made the choice. It is all for nothing, and also all for everything.

I finished *Faith* a few years ago, and felt that the whole series had come to a satisfying conclusion. I was ready to leave the story behind. A few months later, after moving to a different suburb, I was telling my sister about some of the funny things I noticed in my new place. We are far more receptive to things that are different when we first move somewhere. The longer we are there, the less we see. My sister said, "You will be able to use all that in your next story."

At that stage, I wasn't thinking about writing any more fiction. Nevertheless, a week or so later, I started writing a story with brand new characters, in a totally different environment to the endearing seaside village of Waldmeer (Lorne, Victoria, in real life). While Waldmeer is the sort of place anyone would want to live, in terms of beauty and peace, the city suburb of Pittown was the opposite. *Pittown* had begun its journey and, in my mind, was going to be Book 1 of *Something* (yet to be decided). Once the new characters were firmly established (two-thirds of the way into the book), it suddenly became clear that *Pittown* wasn't Book 1 of *Something*. It was, in fact, Book 5 of *Waldmeer*. It was the first I knew of it. It hadn't even crossed my mind. Trust the journey. It will have its own energy. We only need to totally devote ourselves to whatever we are doing and our various paths will make their own way forward.

Two years, another move, and two *Waldmeer* books later, I was packing up boxes for a recent move into an apartment. When you are raising a family, you acquire a lot of stuff. Much of it is helpful in making a warm, interesting home for everyone. However, this was my third opportunity to downsize and each time had been a big clearing. Rather monkish by nature, I was happily taking very little this move. There are always a few things that would be our last material possessions to part with. They are usually worthless, but not to us. Like most mothers, they include special presents from children.

One item was a tealight candle holder, from my eldest son, when he went overseas independently for the first time. Another was also a tealight candle holder from my youngest son. It was his first ever present to me with his own money and own thought. Boys must find tealight candle holders to be economical mother-type-presents.

Another item was a blue, stained-glass, half-moon mobile from my daughter, with her first pay, at age fifteen. It cost half her wage. She got paid, immediately went a few doors

64

down, bought it, and proudly brought it home. Her economics has improved since then. It's called survival.

Another valued possession was a gift from my parents, when I was about twelve. It was glass bookends with an image of praying hands and the *Serenity Prayer*.

> *God, grant me the serenity to accept the things I cannot change, courage to change the things I can, and wisdom to know the difference.*

Those days, most kids didn't have a lot. Families were bigger, and we didn't have cheap, throwaway products. The few special things we had were treasured. Of course, it was no accident that the prayer, the praying hands, and the bookends must have already been finding a way out of me as a future spiritual author.

When I showed a friend a photo of the special gifts, she said, "The light shines through all the chosen items – like you."

In the Wardrobe

A few years after starting the *Waldmeer Series,* I had the idea to record myself reading each chapter and upload it with the blog posts. Those recordings, on YouTube, have now had more than 300,000 views. That's a lot of views for videos which are entirely audio. They also have an excellent retention rate of listening. More often than not, YouTube videos are abandoned after the first ten seconds as customers become accustomed to being entertained with high-paced visual effects.

I had lots of initial technical problems recording the audio on my iPad. The set up could not have been more basic. Some of the problems worked out with experience – don't speak too close to the microphone, don't mumble, watch out for p-sounds, speak clearly, speak naturally, keep the energy up, if it starts droning then stop recording.

In the case of spiritual narrators, it is extremely important to remember that your voice is transferring your healing message to the audience. It is not by magic. Nor does it happen automatically. You must be in the right state of consciousness to convey the elevating, healing energy. If it's not in you, at that moment and every moment of recording, then it certainly will not get transferred to the listener. I find that most professional narrators are not a good match for spiritual books because they do not (and do not profess to) understand and carry the spiritual knowledge fully enough. Acting ability and articulation are important, but energetic transfer is more important.

After my move to a suburban unit, a few years ago, I had the added problem of traffic as it was on a busy road. Every room was noisy. I even tried the toilet which was much quieter but too echoey. So, my new recording studio ended up being my wardrobe. It was the only quiet space, and the clothes absorbed the sound and gave a nice, soft recording voice. Lucky, I'm small!

Friends with Different Names

One of the wonderful things about writing fiction is that we have complete freedom to be as honest and blunt as we feel is necessary to get across an idea. The reader never knows which bits of a story are fictitious and which are true. There is an immunity to story writing which nonfiction does not have. The latter can, generally, not maintain the same sort of freedom due to concerns of hurting others or defamation lawsuits.

Fiction writers tend to use people they know, or have known, as the basis for various characters in their books. It may be only one particular part of someone or an event which is used. Other times, the real-life character is so perfect in his or her ability to represent themselves that no change is deemed necessary or advisable. It is natural for writers to use their own experiences as that is how we make sense of life and relate to other people.

Having said that, I do not think writing is a rational or deliberate process. I never decide who is in my stories. That would be like deciding who we are going to have a relationship with. With nearly eight billion people in the world, would it not be wise to let Life decide who of those people belong with us? With an infinite number of ideas swirling around, would it not be wise to let Life decide which of those ideas belong with us? Stories write themselves, if we let them.

Writing fiction is a joint venture. The people we, directly or vaguely, base our characters on *help* us to write by adding their unique energy to the creation of a story. It is not just the energy that subtlely comes from recalling someone. Rather, it is the actual life-force that radiates from that person. It is a powerful use of an individual's life energy. It is co-creation. Life is a mass of intricate, intertwined energy systems. Their seeming invisibility does not negate their reality or power.

Permission

Characters form in our stories from bits (or all) of people we have met, loved, hated, feared, admired, been jealous of, been disgusted by, and every other imaginable emotional reaction. How else could we write about people except by the life experiences we have had? Obviously, we do not want people to be publicly recognisable, for their sake and ours. So, it is crucial to disguise the identity of anyone.

I have always found it interesting and amusing that no matter how you disguise a person, if they happen to read it, they tend to recognise themselves easily and accurately. They unconsciously know themselves, their characteristics, and the sorts of relationships they have. It is somewhat reassuring that if you have used the negative aspects of someone you know, the person cannot come to you and say, "How dare you use me badly in your story?" Of course, you would say, "But, my dear, why on Earth, do you think that nasty character is you?"

On a more serious note, the point is not to hurt anyone. Although we can laugh at the foibles of others, and even more at our own shortcomings and peculiarities, everyone must be seen with the same love and compassion. We have to be honest, and sometimes brutally so, if we want to get to the crux of any issue. However, the purpose is never to damage. It is always to spiritually, emotionally, and mentally educate. It is to awaken and inspire.

If we are using the life energy of people we know for writing purposes, then isn't it polite to ask permission? No, we can't do that. It's best that people don't know, for sure, if we are talking about them. We want them to take whatever they think relates to them, as a student of life, and work with that by free choice, their own choice, not what someone else has decided for them.

There is a definite sense of caution and duty in regards the involvement of someone else's energy in our story writing. In the wrong hands, using someone known to an author could have a significant, adverse mental and spiritual impact on that person. They probably wouldn't even know where it came from. In the right hands, using someone known to an author could have a significant beneficial impact on them. It is not to be taken lightly. It is certainly not a game. It is a sobering responsibility.

For this reason, I never personally decide who is in my stories. I only use who the guides tell me to use because I can then be confident that the person will be safe and blessed if they happen to suspect their connection to my writing world. From the point of view of the person, I believe, at some level, they have unconsciously agreed to the assignment. It is greatly to their benefit to do so.

Sometimes, people we know will think that we are specifically talking about them, when we are not. I find that this particularly happens in nonfiction when people commonly say things like, *You wrote that for me, didn't you? You must have been thinking about me. That was written about my situation, wasn't it? How did you know what I was thinking? You must have got in my head. I can't believe you know me so well.*

People are way less unique than they think they are. Almost every trait that they have will be shared, in different proportions, by almost everyone they know. In this sense, what applies to one, applies to all, in varying degrees. We

71

want people to apply what we write, to themselves, in whatever way they deem appropriate.

Growth and Relationships

The two most important areas of focus in the writing of the *Waldmeer Series* have been spiritual growth and relationships. *Spiritual growth* because that is the whole point of life. *Relationships* because that is what people think is the whole point of life.

As is told to us in *Waldmeer* (Book 1), *Most of our battle is asking the right question. Growth always requires the questioning of one's current position.* Much further down the track, in *Pittown (Book 5),* we are still being told, *Before anyone can improve their life, they must get the idea that change is possible, that life can be different and better, and that it is worth the effort it takes to make it happen.*

Rather than giving answers outright, which would be ineffective and storyless, much of the series is spent raising questions and demonstrating the problems that need question-asking. We are assured, many times, *Healing has its own power and, once started, moves ahead methodically knowing exactly what track to take for the most efficient and effective results (Waldmeer, Book 1).*

Every relationship automatically pushes towards its own evolution. Each carries its own lessons and purpose. None will fail to fulfil their healing function. It may seem that they can fail, and sometimes fail abysmally. However, healing is inevitable and simply a matter of time. What does the spiritual journey matter other than it transforms our lives? Nowhere is this more obvious than in our personal relationships.

I know, in my heart, that anyone who immerses themselves in the *Waldmeer* journey will be changed in significant ways. I know it because of where the words have come from. I know it because I can see the effect that the series has had on those who have thrown themselves, or tiptoed, into it. For me, this is a great pleasure, satisfaction, and motivation to keep writing. If needed, I would write for one person. Fortunately, more than one person benefits from my work, but one would be enough.

East-West Lead

It would certainly be remiss of me not to tell you that there is an undeniable link between the *Waldmeer Series* and *A Course in Miracles*.

Although I have known about and read *A Course in Miracles* since I was in my early twenties, it was never a primary influence. It was there, in the background, along with all the other treasured books that supported my spiritual studies. However, about five years ago, I received the three audiobooks of *A Course in Miracles* (the Text, Workbook, and Manual for Teachers) through a free offer. Never has anything worth so much been bought for so little.

I started listening to the three audiobooks, one after another, every day, during my walks. When I finished one cycle, I would start again. *A Course in Miracles* is one of those books which has so much in it, that it is always new. All these years later, I will still hear something and think, *I haven't heard that before.* Unless the information is magically changing and updating, then it must be that it is so inspired that it seems ever-fresh and renewing. My listening to ACIM started at the same time as my repairman-messenger appeared. I cannot say it more truthfully than to say, I have always felt the voice that speaks through ACIM is also guiding and manifesting itself in the *Waldmeer Series.* "Something lovely for the world" was born from something else lovely for the world.

Later, another very important influence entered the arena. At the beginning of *Prana (Book 6).* I began seriously listening to Indian guru and mystic, Sadhguru. You will see a definite introduction of new spiritual ideas in *Prana* and continuing through *Purnima (Book 7)*. Even the names of the books took on a Sadhguru-slant.

There we have it – the meeting of East and West through Sadhguru and *A Course in Miracles*. My job is to listen and write. I don't mind, of all the brilliant spiritual beings, who takes the lead. I'm happy that they do!

About the Author

Donna shares her love for the Divine and the world with a large international audience.

All links https://linktr.ee/donnagoddard

Ratings and Reviews

If you have enjoyed this book, I would be most grateful for any ratings/reviews on Amazon or elsewhere. Thank you.

Printed in Great Britain
by Amazon